Is It Art?

Graffiti

Alix Wood

W
FRANKLIN WATTS
LONDON•SYDNEY

Franklin Watts

First published in Great Britain in 2015 by The Watts Publishing Group

Copyright © Alix Wood Books
Produced for Franklin Watts by Alix Wood Books www.alixwoodbooks.co.uk

Editor: Eloise Macgregor
Designer: Alix Wood

Photo Credits:
Cover, 13, 28 © Neale Cousland/Shutterstock; 1 © Pavel L Photo and Video/Shutterstock;
4, 5, 6, 8, 11, 16, 17, 18 top, 20, 21, 26, 27 © Shutterstock; 7 © Awesome Clean Graffiti
Hd Wallpapers; 9 © Mihai Maxim/Shutterstock; 10 © Alix Wood; 12 © Dfrg.msc; 14
© Alfonso d'Agostino/Shutterstock; 15 © Radoslaw Lecyk/Shutterstock; 18 bottom
© David Shankbone; 19 © Steve Mann/Shutterstock; 22 inset public domain; 22
main © catwalker/Shutterstock; 23 left © Oleg Golovnev/Shutterstock; 23 right © lev
radin/Shutterstock; 24 © Andreas Thum, 25 © Cutiekatie; 29 © Sandy Maya Matzen/
Shutterstock

Franklin Watts
An imprint of
Hachette Children's Group
Part of The Watts Publishing Group
Carmelite House
50 Victoria Embankment
London EC4Y 0DZ

Dewey number 709

ISBN 978 1 4451 4396 5

Printed in China

An Hachette UK Company

www.hachette.co.uk
www.franklinwatts.co.u

Contents

What is graffiti?

Graffiti is writing or drawing on walls in public spaces. The style usually involves large lettering, often done using really bold and colourful shapes. It is against the law to paint on walls in most public spaces. Some cities allocate walls especially for graffiti artists to do their art on, though. Graffiti-style art is used in other ways too, not just on walls. Fashion, album covers and logos, for example, often use a graffiti style.

Many people think that graffiti is not real art. They think it makes a place look messy and uncared for. People associate graffiti with crime. If graffiti is painted without permission then it is a crime. Most people would be very angry if someone spray-painted the side of their home! Do you think graffiti lettering, or 'writing' as it is usually called, can be called art?

Arty Fact

Graffiti has been around for several thousand years. There are examples on monuments in ancient Egypt, ancient Greece, and ancient Rome!

Many graffiti artists design their own 'tag'. A tag is usually based on a person's name. Often the letters are so **stylised** you can't read them!

Graffiti: From the Italian, plural of graffito [scribbling; graffito, a scratch]: usually unauthorised writing or drawing on a public surface.

There are many different definitions of what people think art is. Which of these do you agree with?

Art is:
- anything that an artist calls art

- something that is created with imagination and skill. It must be either beautiful, or express important ideas or feelings

- a mixture of 'form' (the way something is created) and 'content' (the 'what' that has been created)

WHAT DO YOU THINK?

A skilful painting of a flower can be called art. It doesn't express important ideas or feelings, though. A political slogan drawn on a wall isn't particularly beautiful, but it may make you think. Which is art? Or are they both art?

Do you think this graffiti makes the area look better or worse?

What is vandalism?

Vandalism is when someone deliberately damages public or private property. Graffiti is an act of vandalism, if it is done without the permission of the owner of the wall. Making an attractive area look ugly surely can't be art?

If we believe that art should be something that is created with imagination and skill, and is either beautiful or expresses important ideas or feelings, then the graffiti in this photo on the left is not art. Most graffiti is considered ugly and lacks both imagination and skill.

WHAT DO YOU THINK?

Would it be better to think of graffiti as having two types; legal graffiti and illegal graffiti? Perhaps then we could say that the legal type is art and any illegal graffiti is vandalism?

The word 'vandal' comes from the ancient Germanic people called the Vandals, who destroyed the beautiful city of Rome when they attacked it in 455.

Clean graffiti, or reverse graffiti, is almost the opposite of vandalism! Artists remove dirt from surfaces to form a picture or words. Using a finger to write 'clean me' on a dirty van is a kind of reverse graffiti. Graffiti artists use a cloth or a high-powered washer for large works. The act of cleaning something isn't illegal, but if it results in creating an image on someone else's property it may be seen as **trespassing**. Someone would have to clean the rest of the wall to get rid of it.

Clean graffiti on a wall in San Francisco's Broadway tunnel by graffiti artist 'Moose'. His art turned the unwelcoming tunnel into a forest. Perhaps this was how the area looked before the tunnel was built?

Arty Fact

Even some companies have started using reverse graffiti to create free advertising. Companies like the **eco-friendly** nature of just using a **stencil** and a power washer. They also don't have to pay for the space!

Does it matter 'what'?

Does what a graffiti artist paints make a difference to whether graffiti is art or not? Does an image have to be beautiful to be called art? And who decides if it is beautiful? Different people have very different ideas about what are nice colours, or attractive images.

PLATE C

Graffiti artists have painted on trains in the image above and in the photograph on page 9. On the train above, the artist has sprayed a signature tag. On the train on page 9, the artist is creating an image of a steam engine on the side of the train. Which one is more creative? Are they both art?

WHAT DO YOU THINK?

Around the world, city transport organisations have to spend a lot of money cleaning graffiti from trains. Most people don't think it looks good and don't want to see it. If the art was nicer to look at, would it be OK to leave it?

This graffiti artist is taking part in a festival in Bucharest, Romania.

The graffiti artist above has chosen a subject that makes you think about the history of trains. Perhaps he is saying that without old steam trains we wouldn't have new trains? Do you think this painting makes the viewer think more about why the artist chose his subject than the image on page 8?

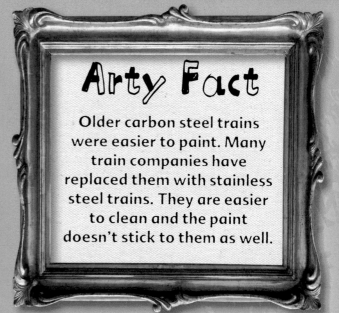

Arty Fact

Older carbon steel trains were easier to paint. Many train companies have replaced them with stainless steel trains. They are easier to clean and the paint doesn't stick to them as well.

Does it matter 'where'?

Does where graffiti is painted make a difference as to whether graffiti is art or not? Some towns and cities have special walls that they invite graffiti artists to paint onto. Other places hold festivals where graffiti artists can come and share their work with others. This graffiti is welcomed and appreciated. The graffiti artists have time to create a special work, instead of hurrying to get it finished before they get caught!

An organised graffiti festival in Cornwall. Artists are invited to come and paint on specially erected boards. The artists exchange tips and admire each other's work. The festival is enjoyed by the whole community.

Graffiti on the walls of an abandoned house.

Spraying graffiti onto someone's home is a criminal offence. The owner of the house will have to pay to get the graffiti painted over. It makes the house and the neighbourhood look uncared for. Most people would prefer to live in an area that doesn't have graffiti all over the walls.

WHAT DO YOU THINK?

Imagine that a graffiti artist sprayed the exact same picture on the side of an attractive building and on a wall specially made for graffiti artists. Are both the paintings art? Are neither of them art? Or is one of them art and the other vandalism?

When an area has a lot of graffiti, people tend to view it as a bad neighbourhood. Property values can go down and crime may increase.

Street art in Melbourne

Melbourne, the second largest city in Australia, has become a centre for street art. The Melbourne Stencil Festival is held every year. The festival lasts for ten days and has exhibitions and workshops. Artists give demonstrations and street art related films are shown. It has become a popular event in the city.

The city of Melbourne encourages street art in certain areas of the city. They do not encourage tags, though. The message to 'do art not tags' is taught in primary schools. The campaign explains the differences between tagging and street art. Tags are beginning to disappear from the area as people agree that street art is art, and tagging is just vandalism.

WHAT DO YOU THINK?

In Melbourne, a stencil by the famous street artist, Banksy, was accidentally painted over by council workers. Some people now want the city's graffiti to be protected. Others think that street art is not meant to last and should not be protected. What do you think?

An amazing piece of street art by artist Adnate on a wall in Melbourne, Australia.

Street artist Adnate moved from painting typical graffiti to doing lifelike faces of the indigenous Australian people. He is now paid to create his art, and has worked all around the world.

Does it matter 'why'?

● Is it important why an artist paints graffiti? If art should be something that expresses important ideas or feelings, it makes sense that we should try and understand what message an artist is trying to put across. A lot of graffiti contains **political** messages. Even the act of graffiti itself is a rebellion against the idea of property and ownership.

Graffiti can be a way to get a message to many people. Advertising posters use wall space in public areas to sell products and services to people. Some graffiti artists use the same wall space to spread ideas to people instead.

WHAT DO YOU THINK?

Is it right that advertisers use public walls to give us messages, while graffiti artists can't? Some graffiti artists argue that they should be allowed to use the walls, too. But advertisers pay to put their messages up. Who is right?

The Berlin Wall in Germany separated West and East Berlin between 1961 and 1989. It was built to stop free movement between the two separate countries of East Germany and West Germany. This graffiti sprayed on the wall saying "the world's too small for walls" is a powerful statement.

Not all graffiti is just people's tags sprayed onto a train. **Thought-provoking** graffiti can make people stop and reassess how they think. Does that make it art? It is still vandalism.

The British graffiti artist known as Banksy visited San Francisco in 2010 and stenciled this graffiti piece on a building on Mission St. The artist often incorporates signs already on a wall. This graffiti shows the **irony** of the 'no trespassing' sign. Are the people who own the building now actually the trespassers?

Arty Fact

Graffiti sprayed on a public wall is seen by more people than if it was in a gallery or a book. In countries with no **freedom of speech** it is an important way for people to anonymously get a message across to many people.

Banksy

Banksy is one of the best-known graffiti artists. He uses humour in his work. His art usually contains a political message. Not everyone appreciates his art, though. One New York mayor called him a vandal and he was wanted by the New York police department because of the graffiti he did while visiting the city.

Banksy has been accepted by many mainstream art lovers, though. He has held exhibitions. His work includes sculptures and a video that Banksy had directed called *Exit Through the Gift Shop*. His artwork has become so collectable that people have been known to drill around pieces and remove sections of a wall to steal the art!

Arty Fact

The mural below is called *Slave Labour*. It is believed to be a protest against child labour used to make items sold to celebrate the Queen's Diamond Jubilee and the 2012 London Olympics.

This Banksy piece was stenciled onto the side of a shop in London. It was later covered with a sheet of perspex to protect it from vandals. The **mural** mysteriously disappeared and was put up for sale at an auction house in Miami, USA! The London community protested and it was withdrawn from sale. It was later sold at a London auction for over £800,000!

No one knows who Banksy really is. If his identity was known he might be arrested. There was speculation that he might be a man called Robin Cunningham, described by a former friend as being a talented artist. In an interview Banksy said "anyone described as being 'good at drawing' doesn't sound like Banksy to me!"

ONE NATION UNDER CCTV

In London, Banksy convinced this building's owners that the wall needed repair. He put up scaffolding behind the security fence, watched by a CCTV camera! Hidden behind a polythene sheet he painted this comment on the '**Big Brother**' society. The piece was painted over despite attempts to save it.

Graffiti and design

Advertising agencies and manufacturers sometimes use graffiti artists to help with their designs. Several graffiti artists offer their services as designers. They can work on projects for computer games, magazine illustrations and skateboard designs, for example.

Frank Shepard Fairey is a street artist with an art degree who started out working in a skateboard shop. Fairey designed a poster supporting Barack Obama's presidential campaign. Fairey made three versions of the poster, with either the words 'hope', 'change' or 'progress' written on them. Fairey distributed hundreds of thousands of stickers and posters, paid for with money from sales of the poster. Fairey received a letter from Barack Obama thanking him for his support.

Fairey's iconic design became an important symbol during the election.

18

Arty Fact

Graffiti artists are using their talents to achieve business success. A New York group called the King of Murals has helped design advertising campaigns to promote brands such as Coca-Cola and M&M's. They have worked on murals for schools and hospitals too.

Graffiti tagging is a little like advertising. The tag is the ad and the writer is the company.

WHAT DO YOU THINK?

Advertisements are designed to appeal to the tastes of that product's **target customer**. What kind of people would respond to graffiti in advertising do you think? What products would use that art style to appeal to their target market?

Graffiti-style artwork is often use to give cars a customised paint job. This VW Beetle was painted to publicise a charity fundraising event.

Develop your style

Try designing your own graffiti on a piece of paper. First you need to choose a style. Do you want to try tagging, or a throw-up? Do you want to paint a piece, or maybe try some wildstyle? Graffiti has its own language, look at the definitions of all these words below and then choose a style that you want to try.

Tagging is the simplest graffiti. It is the writer's **street name** done in one colour.

A *throw-up* is more complicated than a tag, using two or three colours. They're often done using bubble letters in one colour with a different colour outline.

A *blockbuster* covers a large area using a simple design. It is often done in large block letters using paint rollers.

Wildstyle is very stylised writing and is not easy to read. It often features arrows, spikes and curves. They often look **three-dimensional**.

A *piece* is short for 'masterpiece'. It is much more complex and has at least three colours.

A *stencil* is created by spraying paint through a pre-cut stencil.

To develop your own tag, first think up a name that you want to be known by. Write the name in simple letters first. Then try experimenting with the shapes. Try making the letters as if they had been made out of balloons perhaps, or out of planks of wood. Try outlining the letters, or joining some of them together. Have fun until you get a design that you like.

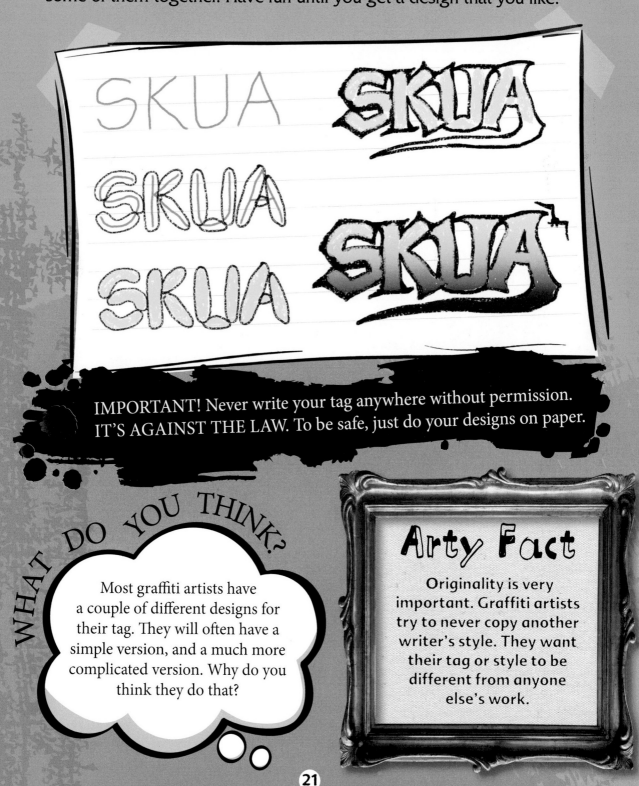

IMPORTANT! Never write your tag anywhere without permission. IT'S AGAINST THE LAW. To be safe, just do your designs on paper.

WHAT DO YOU THINK?

Most graffiti artists have a couple of different designs for their tag. They will often have a simple version, and a much more complicated version. Why do you think they do that?

Arty Fact

Originality is very important. Graffiti artists try to never copy another writer's style. They want their tag or style to be different from anyone else's work.

Graffiti fashion

Graffiti designs are often used in the fashion industry. Skateboarders' clothes and shoes frequently have street art designs on them. Some of the big fashion houses, such as Louis Vuitton and Vivienne Westwood have featured graffiti-inspired designs.

At fashion designer Manish Arora's 2013 Paris show, the stage was brought to life by Paris graffiti artists Vision, Rude and Brok. While the models strutted down the runway, the writers, dressed in black hoodies, created a piece with the words 'Life Is Beautiful' behind them! It was a great bit of publicity for the graffiti-inspired fashion Arora had created and was a perfect backdrop for the clothes.

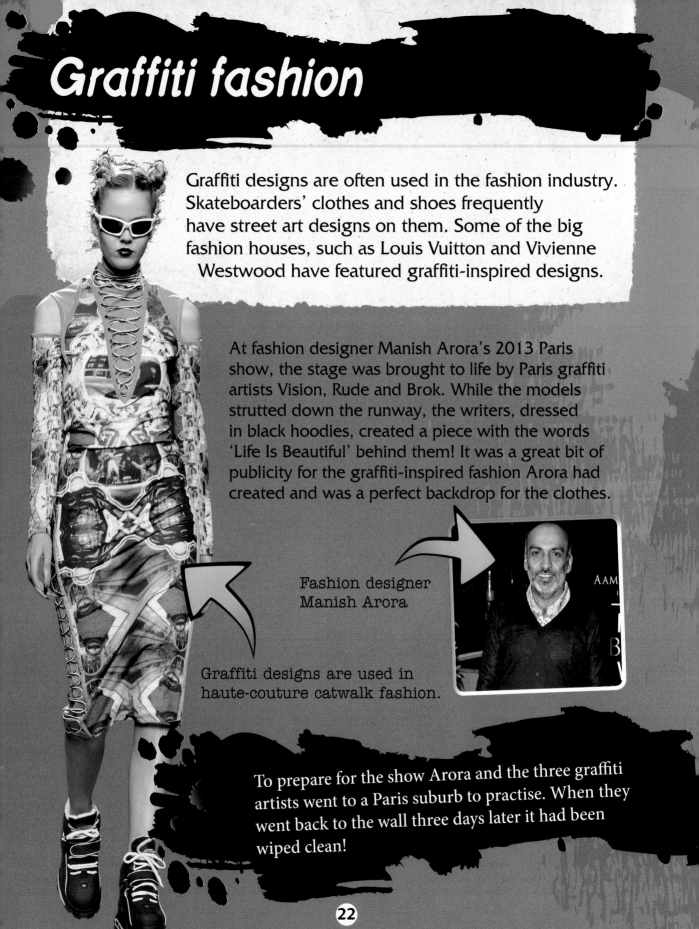

Fashion designer Manish Arora

Graffiti designs are used in haute-couture catwalk fashion.

To prepare for the show Arora and the three graffiti artists went to a Paris suburb to practise. When they went back to the wall three days later it had been wiped clean!

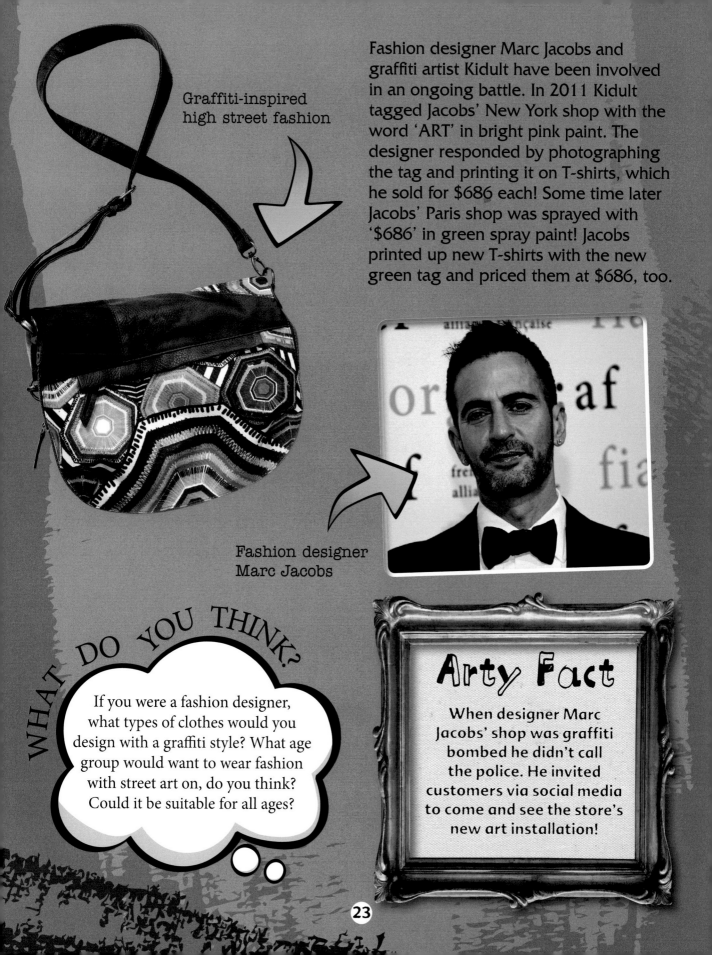

Graffiti-inspired high street fashion

Fashion designer Marc Jacobs and graffiti artist Kidult have been involved in an ongoing battle. In 2011 Kidult tagged Jacobs' New York shop with the word 'ART' in bright pink paint. The designer responded by photographing the tag and printing it on T-shirts, which he sold for $686 each! Some time later Jacobs' Paris shop was sprayed with '$686' in green spray paint! Jacobs printed up new T-shirts with the new green tag and priced them at $686, too.

Fashion designer Marc Jacobs

WHAT DO YOU THINK?

If you were a fashion designer, what types of clothes would you design with a graffiti style? What age group would want to wear fashion with street art on, do you think? Could it be suitable for all ages?

Arty Fact

When designer Marc Jacobs' shop was graffiti bombed he didn't call the police. He invited customers via social media to come and see the store's new art installation!

Keith Haring

Art school graduate Keith Haring became known by the pop art style graffiti that he painted in the New York subways. Haring went on to have his own exhibitions and paint murals in cities all around the world. His work was very varied. He designed a jacket worn by the singer Madonna. He designed lively murals to go on the walls of public hospitals.

Some of Haring's early work was drawn on the black paper rectangles put over empty advertising panels on subway station walls. Haring used white chalk to create simple pictures. He drew dancing figures, a crawling infant with rays of light coming from it, a barking dog, a flying saucer and people with televisions for heads! His drawings got him attention. He was arrested for vandalism several times!

WHAT DO YOU THINK?

Haring had gone to Berlin to paint a mural on the Berlin Wall that separated the **communist** East Berlin from the West. Do you think these fighters (left) might symbolise the struggle between the East and the West?

This statue, *Boxers*, was created when Haring visited Berlin. It stands in an important public square.

Tuttomondo (meaning 'the whole world') was Keith Haring's last work. It was painted onto a church in Pisa, Italy.

Haring always wanted to make his art accessible to everyone. He opened a store that sold posters, T-shirts and other cheap items so that anyone could own his work if they wanted to.

Art for art's sake

● Graffiti artists get up in the middle of the night and head out in the dark to a lonely area. They have planned out their piece and have to work quickly to create it. They make no money from their art, and they don't win any prizes. They could go to jail if they are caught. Why do they do it?

Graffiti artists are not motivated by fame. If anyone finds out who they are they risk going to prison. They are not driven by money, as no one pays them for their work.

Even well-known graffiti artists such as Banksy do not receive money for their walls, as they do not own the walls! Other people will sometimes profit from selling a work that they have done, but the artist needs to stay anonymous. Does this make them the purest artists? They are not driven by greed, just a desire to paint?

'Art for art's sake' was an 19th century French slogan. It means that art should not have to have meaning and purpose. The only aim of a work of art is the self-expression of the artist who created it.

Calling graffiti artists 'the purest artists' makes them sound heroic. But do you think drawing on someone's house is heroic? Just because an artist thinks their work is worthwhile, that doesn't mean that everyone does. Graffiti is illegal for a reason.

Doesn't it make more sense to create art that people actually want, in a place where they want to see it? Painting onto paper or a skateboard means that you can take your picture with you if you move, or sell it more easily to someone else.

Cleaning up graffiti is expensive and time-consuming.

Is graffiti art?

Have you made up your mind? Is graffiti art? To help you, have a look at some of these arguments 'for' and 'against'.

Graffiti IS Art

- Graffiti can deliver important messages

- It can be a way for people to share their ideas freely

- It can help to improve the look of an area

- The artists are expressing themselves

- Museums and galleries are now considering graffiti as art and exhibiting it

- Really great graffiti can attract tourists from around the world

- Some graffiti artists become regular artists and designers using their graffiti style

Graffiti ISN'T Art

- Just signing your name isn't art

- Graffiti can make an area look ugly

- People don't like the look of graffiti and have to spend money to clean it off

- Why should it be up to graffiti artists to decide what our streets look like?

- Graffiti on public property is vandalism

- If graffiti was artistic why has it been made illegal?

- Graffiti artists have to do their work quickly and can't take time and trouble over their art

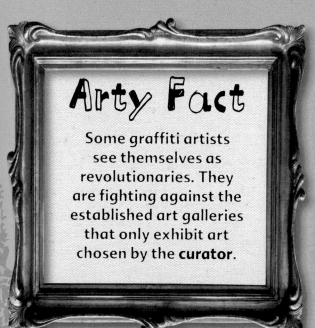

Arty Fact

Some graffiti artists see themselves as revolutionaries. They are fighting against the established art galleries that only exhibit art chosen by the **curator**.

Do you think that if Picasso had painted his work on the side of a train instead of on a canvas, it would still be art?

Graffiti artists have many different styles and approaches to what they do. Some are very political in their messages. Some prefer to create images that amaze or inspire. Other artists just want to leave their mark around the world. Perhaps as long as enough people appreciate the work that a graffiti artist does, it doesn't matter if other people don't rate them as an artist?

WHAT DO YOU THINK?

If you are not sure, that's OK. Perhaps some graffiti could be called art and some couldn't? Which artists or types of graffiti do you think could be called art?

Glossary

Big Brother
An all-powerful government or organisation monitoring and directing people's actions, from a storyline in a book by George Orwell.

communist
A person or state who believes in communism or is a member of a political party that supports communism.

curator
A person in charge of a gallery, museum or zoo.

eco-friendly
Not harmful to the environment.

freedom of speech
The political right to communicate one's opinions and ideas.

irony
The use of words that mean the opposite of what one really intends.

mural
A painting applied to and made part of a wall surface.

political
Of or relating to a government or the conduct of government.

stencil
A piece of material, such as a sheet of paper, with lettering or a design that is cut out and through which ink or paint is forced onto a surface to be printed.

street name
The name a graffiti artist calls themselves so that they remain anonymous.

stylised
Something that is represented or designed according to a style or pattern rather than according to nature or tradition.

target customer
A group of customers towards which a business has decided to aim its marketing efforts and its merchandise.

thought-provoking
Something that stimulates interest or thought.

three-dimensional
Giving the appearance of depth or varying distances.

trespassing
To enter unlawfully onto land owned by someone else.

For more information

Books

Gogerly, Liz. Radar: Art on the Street: *Graffiti Culture*. London, UK: Wayland, 2013.

Storey, Rita. EDGE: Street: *Art*. Franklin Watts, 2013.

Uzi. *Graffiti Coloring Book*. Årsta, Sweden: Dokument, 2009.

Websites

Tate Gallery
http://kids.tate.org.uk/games/street-art/
Great website designed for kids with an interest in art. Interactive site where you can create your own graffiti.

Haring Kids
http://www.haringkids.com
An interactive colouring book where you can create graffiti pictures using some of Keith Haring's most famous images.

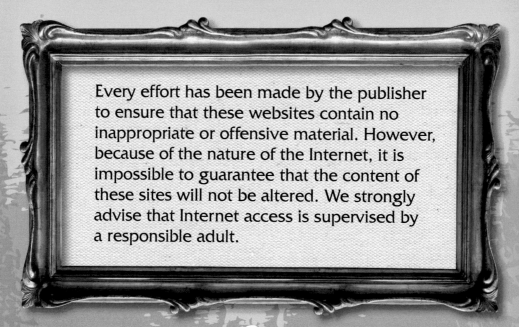

Every effort has been made by the publisher to ensure that these websites contain no inappropriate or offensive material. However, because of the nature of the Internet, it is impossible to guarantee that the content of these sites will not be altered. We strongly advise that Internet access is supervised by a responsible adult.

Index